MW00653800

Journey of a Thought:
The Antidote!

STEVEN BRITT-EL

Published in the United States
by Writer's Tablet Publishing Agency
Marietta, Georgia
www.Writerstablet.org

Copyright © 2021 Steven Britt-El

All rights reserved. This book or any portion thereof may not be
reproduced or used in any manner whatsoever without the express
written permission of the publisher except for the use of brief quotations
in a book review.

ISBN: 978-0-578-28949-6

DEDICATION

This book is dedicated to my beloved grandmother Glenora Britt.
Your gift of love will forever live.
Rest in peace.

My beautiful mother, Roselyn Britt. So many of my resurrections
wouldn't have been possible without you. Thank you for being my
Earth!!

Thanks to my father (The General) for introducing me to the Moorish
Circle 7 and the highest principles known to man, love, truth, peace,
freedom, and justice. Rest in peace, soldier!

A special thanks to Felicia Underwood, who was a fabulous writer
and friend. She always encouraged me to write down my thoughts
and share them with the world.
Rest in peace, my dear friend!

And of course, thanks to my wife, children, and family for always
supporting me and just allowing me to be me.

CONTENTS

CONTROL

Moving in droves
Panic pandemic
Introduced to seduce
The order of your routine
Flesh prisoner
Skin, tight bound to a human being
Gone fishing, out to lunch
You didn't even see them
Holographic illusionist magnificent
Reparations black non-existing
Lost nationality
Militant
Lost position

Read between the scenes illusions of what you imagine you've seen
Three dot triple-beam
Sniper rooftop hundreds killed
CIA or confidential militia team
Bilateral collateral urgently endorses our brand
Free hand government demand

We own you now, Covid 19 saved all y'all's asses
Opened the door, fronted the front man a hand
I saw it though, left-hand pass
Blind mass
New World Order hourglass
Tick tock tick, they hella slick
Chain linked hands up don't shoot!
Light your Bics
Amazon, the new Don chess piece retail defeat
Macy's upside down, three closed down in my hood last week
Stimulate a presidential debate
Lining up to vote
Don't slip!
Reptilians not fake
Demonstrate a democracy
Big mistake

My likes are low
IG, social media look at my flow

JOURNEY OF A THOUGHT

Plastic makeover, please hurry! Deceased on the table
Silicone breasts, malpractice, big butt surgery
Small waist
But left the crooked face
I knew they were the same people; my equal with a different lust
Black Hollywood packed on a star-struck bus
Physical distortion, naw, I'd rather mentally readjust
My brain, not my frame
Exalt your being by loving your name
Queen

USP penal code
Mailman reload
Fed-X, UPS
Factory jobs economy implode
Face recognition
Your badge yellow-vest robot conditions
Not responsible, huh?
Inflation affliction

Barcode neck scan, population decrease; girl to a she-man
No longer impossible, infrared gon' spot you
Manual equivalency test
Incompetent score
Entered this realm but left no fingerprints on the trap door
Let me see your hand apple watch command
Plan B, Siri, and the local Taliban
Europeans rule the New World
Black Pope free the captives from the Catholic Vatican

DNA genetic food play infected meat
Vegan greenhouse hay, no fast-food appetite
Not trying to be a cloned humanite
Just trying to detect these concocted parasites on my plate
Legalized weed, banned guns –
Which is going to conquer your State?
Drug deal decline, pharmaceutical paradigm
War on drugs two decades behind
Line up right here –
Free prescription heroine pills in the doctor's health line
We ain't blind
Just high on weed sprayed with atrazine and a TV couch behind

2

JOURNEY OF A THOUGHT

Politics ballot tricks cast your spell
Energy vampires
House of Reps—I meant house of hell
Pump iron, no reps
Presidential theft
Weak—nothing left
Tougher than Teflon; where's your vest?
Four corner ring, white towel and they sing
Under our roof, but not for the black team
So stay woke, don't dream
Grab hold to the olive branch that grows from our African ravine

Take back no lack, spiritual flight intact
Exact the opposite
Education
Head Start held us back
Pro-black 'cause black self-hate reversed the fight
Some of us denounced our own kin last night
Hate you back
Sentenced to death, our families unite in the pro-black plight

British pirate lick blood demonic
American parasite public ritual
Pro-biotic

Mayweather hype, Deontae Wilder blood sacrifice
And they think we were all born at night
Not quite
Ssshhhh

To be continued…

JOURNEY OF A THOUGHT

I saw a shadow, time to draw veil
Next message you receive will be in Hieroglyphics or
Egyptian braille
Pay attention, don't fall or fail
Underground bunker and I wish you all a wishing well

Wake up!

TO BE

I'm cold
But I'm bold
Baked in an oven
I broke the clay mold
Protoplast dripped through the cracks
Onto my spaceless and faceless face
I shaped form and became bound
To a dwelling place built above ground
But I defied the fall
Angel wings held me in grace
No need to lie on your back or orbit lost in space

Open your eyes, a voice said

But I'm scared
It's dark
I have no knowledge
I haven't been fed

You dripped from a clot
I created you from a thought
 Now go within from inside out
And by the way
Why do you fear and lead with doubt?
Perfect creation
Polluted with worldly infestations
I created you to be ruler over all your determinations
You know not fear
I have whispered in your ear
The truth about what's far and near
You are it; you are this, and that
In fact
You are Thee from front to back
How dare you lack and say you can't?
When I reawaken you
You will see
I haven't forsaken Thee
You will be and do as I do
See as I see
And be I in Thee
Infinitely

5

50 BLOCKS: THE DESTINY

50, to me a number or a mark in time only my grandma dreamt for me
Street shadows and corner boys laughed and showed us all our coffins
and jail cells
To be
How can you become what you can't see or dream?
Overshadowing of project walls and buildings blocked my mental escape
Grandma's flight was the gate

The sun shined but on a crooked fatherless path
Project ghosts were prophets
With reverse light and slick blueprints, 50 seemed not to exist
Grandma's eyes saw differently
Even when I was driving a car with no steering wheel on a crash course
on 14th Street
36 more blocks uptown; man, I'm not gon' make it

Corner boys still grinning, flashing bankrolls beneath the project buildings
Shiny bling replaced the sunlight
I stayed 14 for three years
Lost in time, not even the worst that could be
Seeing Grandma's eyes staring at me
The pain worse than visualizing being under – six feet
18th Street drug block – mob dreams, ghosts, conversations in between
the hustle
So, you him now?
Money over merit I soon would inherit
Grandma knew that too
Smile on her face, angel eyes still pierced my soul
She kept me though in her grace so bold

"Daddy, I'm yours," infant hands grabbing my legs
Project ghosts didn't leave yet
My mother stopped on 14th Street too, but she didn't stay there
I often wondered if she could see over the project walls before me
Your daddy ain't shit! Those ghosts kept telling me
Dropping me on 14th Street instead of a black baby hearse
Trying to make it to 50th Street seemed like a gift
Her eyes didn't have the same light as Grandma's, so I thought I was a
curse

Your daddy ain't shit left me on 14th Street; I'll show him
Success will be the light that would cover all the dirt and lies
You hurt me, not them

JOURNEY OF A THOUGHT

Bubble gum sticky but don't erase permanent ink
Grandma told us not to go to sleep
We see that bald spot in your head Squeak

Mama done well though for me
Did the sun shine more radiant than the rainbow on the other building
from my windows?
Open my eyes to go where? When I could just stay inside my high rise
The thought of not knowing how I was going to get uptown

50th Street bound
Carrying all the lies; fuck it, I'll lamp here and be them
Nope, not gon' work, gotta keep going to the next block
I dropped something on 18th Street (Damn, I made it there!)
Sherita is that you? Grandma told me you were coming, looking like me
too, huh
And y'all said Daddy ain't shit...

One hand on the steering wheel driving off course, still on a crash route
But I saw a little light when I went to Grandma's house
Now I see what this is all about
My gift, my light took me to 25th Street
Them gangsters didn't go nowhere
All cities have a Martin Luther King Street that goes all the way uptown
So where you getting off at?
Grandma didn't lie, same look in her eye
I love you son (a whooping and a hug), you hungry?
You're mine for life so don't you cry, just ride
Still on that unleaded, where you headed
With that irregular plan? A son now, huh? Miracle man
How you gon' stand?

Grandma, I'm on 34th Street
Am I tall now? Do they still hate me down there?
See you soon

Skipped over some blocks where time stood still (you know, college)
Death by assumption consumption, human error outcast, then
Where my father at? What do you mean, *he ain't shit?*
Didn't he help you leave me on 14th Street?
I think?

Still on that bubble gum, made me numb
The problem is mine to deal with – ok, here it comes
My kids going with me,
Mama do you love me?
Why they keep calling me nigger?

7

JOURNEY OF A THOUGHT

Why do we live over here?
Is this the light outside the project walls?
I didn't ask to be here

Those blocks I left off I was traveling in hate, saying
I'll pay them back when I'm bigger, trust that faith
50th Street looks brighter Grandma
The missing pages seemed ageless, I would soon discover
That the blood in my veins dripped from an ageless Mother

"Black man, stand up and take your place," a voice said
Them ghosts and gangstas taught us never scared
Black fist balled up, Timbs laced up tight moving in silence
Now I knew my plight

Oh, you God body now, laughed the streets
Still getting that paper plan understood
Gold king crown glowing from under my hood
Islam, my brother, take back them lost years
Oh shit, that's you? What's up Dad? No more tears of hate
14th Street ain't all that bad, I'll wear that faith

Now here I am two years later
Adding a few verses that I saved for later
50 blocks began a short story
But I have to give my sweet mother all the glory
Held me close and nourished me well
Even while living in a place deemed as hell
The project walls she escaped through strong vision
Moving steady up stream and being firm in her decision
Wow, look at her go; and before anyone knew it
This soon to be mother who graduated from Blewitt
Didn't stop there, she continued with strong dedication
Knowing full well our future would depend on her higher education

Through hardships, trials, and painful adversity
My beautiful mother still graduated from Washington University
I'm so proud of you Ma, your lessons have left a mark in my brain
And have allowed me to share with my kids where I got all my game
52 blocks without you would not have been the same
So I have to give you all the love and glory
Now I can relax and end my story

NOT BY CHANCE

We all have been given a chance
To take our first and last glance
Our stories hold truths of damnation
Our last dance
And our glory
Repeat your story enough and it will sink into the next
Like a download repository

I don't have a college degree
But my journey embodies a wise and strong mental pedigree
Growing up we were taught
The apple doesn't fall far from the tree
I've traveled in the present
Future
And the past
I've seen enough in this life that has shattered my brain like a shotgun
    blast
Desert storm
Mother's arms
Never exempt from worldly harm
Didn't matter the dwelling place
Projects, suburbs, or urban farm
Your life is not by chance
So shuffle the cards and make your own plan

I know you're saying Mama failed me
And Daddy mailed me a letter from the pen
With all this pain and lies, I'm destined not to win
Who am I?
Where did I come from?
What shall I claim?
Are Negro, Black and Colored any different than our family name?
In the days of old you were named by your talents
Should it be any different now?
Do you rebuke who you really are and your family's mentality?
Ups and downs; frowns and smiles
We all have had to handle it
So when you're blessed to take your next glance
Trace yourself back and ask yourself,
Do I really want to trade in my hand?

We come from a place that didn't allow disgrace, failure
Or quitting the race
All taught to stand up, be strong
And take your worldly place

9

JOURNEY OF A THOUGHT

Love was the leader
Big Mama was the feeder
Our parents were the seeders
And you better say, "Yes ma'am" and "Yes sir" whenever you greet
    them
Every soul that entered 2310 and 3818 was reared the same
The principles our family was taught hold more than a tag or a name
If you don't believe me, just look at those who aren't still in the game

Just like hand me downs, they fit like they were brand new
So where do you get off telling me you never had to wear my shoes?
They fit my feet and your feet and even his and hers
Fifty years from now you'll see them still standing on the curb
The cycle of life goes around and around and will repeat itself again
Or maybe you can rub the crystal ball and trade your life back in

At any rate, we all are great
And the apple isn't a sin
The seeders who created you
Prepared us all to win

MENTAL POVERTY

Great magnificent globe
Reveal the untold the unseen
The Code
Of life
Of strife
A perfected way to greater heights
I want to fly above clouds and sing real loud
Bow down my crown
Love, live and not frown
What you mean, be proud?
I give, I've tried
Not perfect
I've lied
Received, I gave, I'm weak
I'm brave
No light, dark cave
Indeed, you're that; but you've killed, you've shamed
The gift I gave has
Power to save
And you've chosen to enslave
Your Spirit, a cage
Your thoughts and brain – Remove those chains!
As I, the Globe, will rotate the same
Destruction and pain repent refrain
I'm trying
It's hard
Tormented and scorned
By worldly tests inflicting my flesh
My mirror shows less the Being I am
The message I missed
Was lost in spam, deleted reality
To live duality
I want to press on
Is this the finale?
Afraid to sleep or die in an alley
I want to live on and on
Black horse and a chariot
My wisdom, I'll share it
To again accept glory and live my heritage

JOURNEY OF A THOUGHT

It's rich, I'll bear it
No complaints
Discernment
My heaven—I'll earn it
My role—I'll learn it, more work, less sermon
Destroy my hermit
Truth changes not and nothing can burn it
Magnificent me, my mind is merit
I'll rewrite my story, unfold
Her Glory, Upload Her Glory
Uphold Her Glory!

LOVE WIND

There are powers in the wind
As it blows again and again
Her scent transcends
As does the music from her playlist begin
Captivating
Manipulating
Spinning me out of control
My soul pierced
Her fire essence
Fierce
She kissed me deeply and bold
Heavy heartbeat
Cold feet
From the kiss that was ever so sweet
The wind blew again
I became a helpless man
I surrendered to her command
One dance
A romance
A Goddess with a sure plan
I grabbed her hand
As we ran to the sand, now a silent band
Just our eyes, the ocean
The Moon a notion
Our bodies collide
A water slide
Her mist
A love potion
Hypnosis, deep motions
High tides now a roaring ocean
Her devotion brought us closer
Her playlist so provoking
She whispered
My King, keep swimming, keep stroking

STRINGS

The web Spider-Man spun
The dial-up had begun
And took what seemed an eternity
But surfing was still fun
Ok, ok, it's about to connect…
And then the phone rung
And yet we sit there with a glare
Into a box that wrapped us up like a tube sock
Or a pile of bills, like
Pay what and when?
I don't care, I just want to be still
And feel real
On the enter the net
I got more info than you
You wanna bet?

What you say?
You read a book and got the same info for free
Time and no telephone line
Surfboard and time
Rewind, rewind
Make it faster!
5g Covid tree
Cyber towers, high speed, and higher fees
They paid with human sacrifice
Just to give faster advice
And Google bullshit got us all on the list
With apps and slaps across the face

No chains this time, just canes for the young
Outside ain't fun
We just want to surf, not build our turf
Play football
WTF is a Nerf?
Besides, I need to erase all the pop ups from my PC
Before I'm hacked and cloned
Spy drones interrupted you and iPhones
Who is that talking?
Thought we were alone
Oh, that's just Siri
Don't be leery

Don't you remember when you self-surrendered your rights to
  privacy?
So don't act blindly
Every time you search, you birth your clone
No need for you
Your thoughts are downloaded and gone
Not to mention
Control-Alt-Delete dimension
Too busy waterless surfing
Caught up in a web
Hard drive locked on social media jive
Virus in your brain
Systems crashed
Apple and Microsoft collide
Hmmm, maybe they joined teams to continue this New World Order
Cyber Pandemic Genocide
Programming a diabolical movement of suicide
And they lied
Oops!
You bit the bait, chip already planted inside
Can't run, can't hide
Death be the answer of an objective nationality rejection
African American Apartheid...

Go figure
Pull the trigger
Firing squad automatic death
Get out of the web before there's nothing left
Could this be the horizon, or the conclusion of a worldly theft?

PERCEPTION

It's peculiar how one word can mean so many things
My dear Creator, I'm trying to decipher what they all mean
My understanding is wrong, it's right
How do I decipher my plight?
I give, I take
But when I don't understand it's my bad, my mistake
Left feeling lost and incomplete
Broken and torn and not knowing when to speak
Revolving, revolving
Trying to resolve what I know I didn't create
But as fate would have it, I don't love; I've been fake
And not one time have I uttered I don't make any mistakes
I just want some food on my plate
I ate when I first opened my gate
No lost love or hate
I'm a king and I was taught to take my place
But not from you, my Queen
You are true and a force in why I lace my boots
In the morning, no scorning, you are adoring
As a King my wish is to make my Queen feel good
I don't like when you feel misunderstood
In your skin I've been, in your heart I trend
I will never leave you, there's no end
A new word, a new sound, a new meaning we shall blend
Sorry love and all the above will shallow what you know I'm made of
For my kingdom was open for you with no push, no shove
Heaven above knew you needed a special hug
And so did I
But initially I understood you first, and heard your silent cry
To be held, to be well and to just be you
I will definitely be present to see you through
I just don't want you to forget I need you too
Not just in your perception, not in "I do for you this way" deception
Just in a loving way of reception

52 BLOCKS: GAME 1

I always thought I could ball
So at 17 I stumbled on the court
Not knowing my soon to be daughter would be my new sport
I can bend the truth, tell a lie
Or even distort
Allah knows I'm thankful her teenage mother was pro-life
And did not abort
Many miles and milestones caused me great grief
I had an altercation in these mean streets
Wasn't present to touch my first-born's new feet
I toughed it out, although broken and torn
I was not present to witness my first born
Sherita Marie Britt-El
My beautiful daughter's birth given name
I am so blessed I was raised by a family who taught me to stay in the
    game
She changed my life, how dear she did
I was only 17
No longer a kid
Responsibilities came with playing this sport
34 years later,
I'm still on the court

I love you, my first born
And I thank Allah you were my first inspiration
Coach
And guide
If anyone ever told you
You didn't save my life
They lied
Rocco and Mecca are reflections of who you taught me to be
When I hear their footsteps, I hear Sherita B

I love you, my first born
So great that you came
Missed critical shots in my first playoff game
But never gave up, still pulling that chain
So always remember your dad loves you dear
And may the sound of my voice stay forever in your ear
So precious to me, my first begotten
You used to be spoiled and a little bit rotten
But that never bothered me nor rocked my world
You're 34 now but still Daddy's little girl
I know where you're at and you know where I've been

JOURNEY OF A THOUGHT

But never expected to create you a twin
If time could go back, I would still play the game
17 years old and would love you the same
Things were different back then, my life was in shams
Even though I was gone, I made sure you were with your fam
They loved you dearly, I longed to be there
I never wanted you to think that Dad didn't care
To prove to myself I was in it for the long haul
Instead of buying J's for myself
I took you to the mall
I know you had tough times and things weren't perfect
No need to ask anyone if your dad loved you
No need to search it

Love you, my first-born princess

Your Loving Father,

Steven Britt-El

BURIED BOOTS

Walk this way man, walk
But the boots don't fit, no grip
Too big
Eight years old
Shadow dad manifesting duality genocide
Infectious transmission, hot girl inhibitions
Lost and found your spermicide

Mother, Mother, Mother

Penitentiary pen
Where I'm going
Man, where you been?
But I gotta get there
I see them way up the hill, shining
Why not me?
What's holding my feet?
Blinding rage
Parental absence, self-made
Me, a treacherous menace
Neighborhood chemist
Devil let me go rock the bells
No baptism
I wasn't sexually present
Teenage mother jizzm injection created me
Disappearance of a first direct descendant of he
Won't be the demise of thee
Although your peers forced your ironclad boots on my childhood feet

Maaannnn, you look just like your daddy!

Got that talk mouthpiece dripping imagery identically
Put me in idolizing bondage
Unholy responses
My feet starting to fit your boots
Do I have a choice?
Another option: neighborhood wall of ink sinking and sinking
Voices in my head repeating, repeating
Gangsta, gangsta
Damn, what the fuck are they yelling?

JOURNEY OF A THOUGHT

Hand slap, mathematical equations
I had a thirsty yellow cab driver looking for me
Man, he over there, why you parallel on me?
His daddy ordered his hearse at birth
Emblematical reversed collateral damage
My path, how fucking suicidal
Boots tighter
Elohim, please lift my soul higher
Desire… desire…

Escalator, I'm running
Project elevator broke
Pow, pow, pow!
Harriet Tubman gunnin'
Duck down, duck down!

Apparatus astral projection
Circle 7 injection
Unread scrolls buried beneath the tunnel
Light appeared – Pops had left them
Mother intercepted the blueprint
My laces loosened
No wrung neck like gooses
And truces were formed
Knowledge swarmed
Gangbanger disarmed – AK47
Rapid tongue, barefoot spitting
High octave lungs

Mother, Mother, Mother

I understood her disdain, the lies
But why—was I left born to die
Confused, mentally abused
I had to write his name
You signed and sang a thousand times
But I guess I had to wear his boots
Flight preparation, heights and pinnacles
No more ink stains
Freedom at last—third eye tentacles
Give me a hug, Mother
I'm propelling, expelling
No more heavy boots
Fifth dimensional melanin dwelling

Be back soon
Can't believe all that saving power was held captive
And you're not even the chaplain
Prisoner of war God
Black Pandora's box lies
The exhuming of a neighborhood pharaoh
We prophesied your rise

Father, Father, Father

Everybody thinks you're wrong
I honor the 7
Rest In Peace
I buried those boots so they wouldn't fit my son's feet
But thanks for the bones and the laces

HER WISH

I want what I want
The time is now
To be enamored by charm
And blind to harm
Illusions of love
Not tight
Not snug
I need a hug
Just something to feel
My time seems short
I gave so long
To what I thought would last forever
To him, whoever
Was clever and keen
I imagined for now
Forsaking my dreams
To wait for truth
A silent King
Who's kind and clear
And endear my essence
The lessons I've failed
Would be his blessings
To hold me tight and love me right
In fear or fright
Of who I am and what I want
He chose, his life is mine for free
For me to give myself to him
A child, a gift
My wish, my choice
His smile rejoiced
My dream is real, he spoke his voice
My king, my king, my unbroken heart

JUST DO IT

Face it head on
Dead on
Let's conquer our foes
Ten toes
Elbows
Highs, lows
Ups, downs
The time is now
No pats
No backs
No crowds
No corner men
White towels
To throw in
Just you
Just I
All truth
No lies
Be strong
Don't cry
      Let's rise
          And fly
              Away

Obey
The lessons we've learned
You've earned
The right
Now use your might
To fight
Through pain
Rename
Reclaim
Your life
Your spirit
      Run to it
          Don't fear it
            Behold
               Endear it

JOURNEY OF A THOUGHT

It's tough
I know
I've fought alone
With help
Without
My spirit remained my will
No doubts
        To win
             To pray
                  To smile
                       To play

With life
In love
In peace
In war
In light
In dark
I'm here
Not far
From you
Be true
To you
        Be still
             To heal
                  The person inside reveal

Reveal
In thought
Cry cloth
The tears
Will fall
No friends
No calls
But silence speaks loud
Your spirit is blocked
        Your noise
             Too loud
                To hear
                  Your fear

JOURNEY OF A THOUGHT

The curse
You bear
It's real
It's strong
Must leave
Be gone
       For good
            From home
                It's time

Not blind
To spells
In tune
To hell
Black magic and spells
           Can't dwell
              Where light
                  Exists

Persist
Prevail
The visions are strong
No singing new songs
           Old history to bury
              Spit out old bones
                Release us now we pray

Okay
Today a new day
No longer lie down
For vultures to prey
           I'm healing
              I'm strong
                My darkness is gone

I own my life
I love me now
My thoughts are clear
           My soul is pure
              I hold the key
                I hold the cure...

QUEEN ESSENTIALS

Her essence, her eyes, her garden, her frame
Her speechless voice revealed her true countenance and name
She spoke with her eyes, and I kneeled to her command
A duty any king would fulfill
It wasn't a demand Intelligent
Graceful
Angelic
Soft spoken
Beautiful but not a token
Goddess God-fearing
Engineering her seeds to perfection
Mind never closed, her spirit open
She pointed, it was done
Mannerable daughters, obedient sons
The stroke of her hand and the sweetness of her breath
Alleviates her Kings pressures by the ton
Speaking softly, vocals like music
Never bossy
A kiss from her honey lips so glossy
I am her King, I'll do anything
Our love is sacred
Forever in her matrix of bliss
Her performance as a queen is exceptional
I attend at once to her honey do list
Gladiator mediator
Diplomatic protector
Forever cherish, relish in your charm
Love lock my arms to lay between what keeps me from harm
You feed the earth and those you birth with natural food; my seeds thirst
Please save me my Queen from my own masculine curse
It's evident all beautiful Heavenly beings came first
And nothing else in this creation can quench a King's thirst

FORGOTTEN KINGS

"Searching for a place," he said to me

Poised and erect, I assumed a wise man to be
Lifestyle worn
He wasn't neat
Shirt stained and torn
Mismatched shoes covered his feet

The approach was subtle
No flexin', no rebuttal
Streetlights on by the bridge near the MLK tunnel

He looked me in my eyes as a father would his son
And thanked me for the handshake
And for not calling him a bum

I could tell by his manners, prolific parables
Words of wisdom
And professed talents
He had been broken down by the systematic government
Lost his job
Lost his balance

We rotated for hours and hours about life
The unseen broken dreams
Heaven and Earth and that which sits in between
Living conditions, food from the mission
And rainwater for a splash of clean

Dazed and amazed by this journeyman
With an ancient caravan
That reflects a magnificent life of a brilliant Superman

Empathy
He didn't need sympathy
He didn't bleed
All he asked was a way to receive
A seat at the table
He wasn't a crook, he wasn't a thief
Misunderstood
Worked diligently
Served my country and community militantly
Wife and kids – took care of them with honor
Splendidly

JOURNEY OF A THOUGHT

Now a broken King under a bridge on MLK
Not begging, refusing to lean
Just wants to be recognized as another human being
Encompassed and equipped to fulfill more dreams
It's not what it seems

I appreciate you listened
I can tell you're strong
Keen, and, too, an intellectual king

As a matter of fact—father, uncle, brother from one mother
We birthed from the same blood clot
Divine dimensions an atomic explosion
A Mother Earth discovery our now dwelling spot of compulsion

I follow you
The hollow truth
I see plainly reversed the knowledge of self and Kings
That originated our names of infinity
We persevere to death and divinity

I admire your shelf-life strife and your will to aspire
Contrary to your belief
You're not the ordinary
And I too have dealt with the same systemic adversaries

I spoke to my elder kindred king with poise
Reciting great quotes of Noble Drew Ali
Marcus Garvey and another great,
W.E.B. Dubois
Up, you mighty Kings!
Accomplish what you will
The blueprint I have doesn't require us to dredge or hurdle the hill

Respectfully united, we move with force zealously
No hatred, no time for jealousy
Scientifically we move methodically

Kings are Kings and dreams are dreams
If we don't respect one another
We will continue to suffer a dying legacy

JOURNEY OF A THOUGHT

I bowed my crown to him and pressed forward majestically
"See you tomorrow, King," he replied
I replied,
Most definitely

52 BLOCKS: GAME 2

17 years in the game
They say practice makes you great
My second child swam hard to make it through the gate
Miracle Baby
The doctors proclaimed
But I know you came here to challenge the game

I swore to myself if God blessed me with a son
I would show my beloved father how it was done
Don't get it twisted – I'm not blasting my pops
He just wasn't there to push me to the top
Wait a minute, that statement isn't all the way correct
He introduced me to Islam
And I began to stand tall, and erect

My Son, you brought new challenges to the game
But I had it all figured out
My playbook was strong 'cause Islam taught me the route
Pops always told me to study my lessons
And when you have a son, pass down these great blessings

So I followed his instructions and honored his authority
People who knew not talked and whispered about my religion
But I didn't care because they were not the majority

Man, oh man, I can't explain how great it is being your father
Sometimes I jump up and down; I even holler
Allah U Akbar
I thank you, my God
My son is a blessing
I think I've done my job

I love you, my strong reflection
My image you will forever be
When your son is born, I hope you will remember me
Pass down the jewels, the lessons, and the game
Raise your flag high and honor our name
While traveling the world stay focused, and never overlook
Just remember, your 52-year-old father gave you the playbook
I love you Prince

Your Loving Father,

Steven Britt-El

30

BIG BROTHER

Big brother, big brother
Why are you so tall?

Because I must hold you up high from the lower world
And from evil things that crawl

Big brother, big brother
Why don't you cry?

Because if I cry
The spirit in you might die

Big brother, big brother
Why do you share?

Because I'd rather give to those in need
And in despair

Big brother, big brother
Why do you teach?

Because the lessons I've learned
Will allow you to reach

Big brother, big brother
Why do you love?

Because where I came from
We were taught to be hard and to be thugs

Big brother, big brother
Why do you work?

Because nothing is free
Not even this earth

Big brother, big brother
How long will you live?

As long as my mind, spirit, and soul
Have something to give

Big brother, big brother
Thank you, Big Brother

BLACK LOVE

Black Love
What is it to you?
How shall I define?
I assumed no matter the love
It should fit like a glove

No, no, no, not the one OJ wore
Wait, wait, wait, don't leave
I am speaking of Black Love

What do you mean I didn't do it right?
Must we argue and fight?
I watch TV and read the books you gave me
See, don't they look happy in Black Love?

Off balance
I'm not them, him, or me
Asking myself is she her, them, or
A mirrored projection of a reflection
Of something that doesn't exist

Black Love
The glove doesn't fit baby
I'm trying, dying to see it; be it
Hold you, love you, mold you
I gave you my heart from the start
Eyes and ears opened
I know I received you because the hair on my arms
Tickled my soul's antennae

Black Love
You're the love, you're the kept secret, you're the glove
Vibrating ethers catch them
They don't speak tongue language
You don't love me, you don't care
I don't even know who you are anymore

Maybe before a morning hug
Black Love before a coffee mug
Roll over, a kiss, let's wear a new glove

So, could it be that the glove couldn't grip, or did reality slip?

My mama said, *Well hell*
My daddy said, *Black Love*
The glove
Mine fits me far beyond what you see
Give her glove back and wear your own
Black Love glove
Then you'll see the essence of self-expression

COMMA DRAMA

Child support
We will definitely extort
Minimum wage fathers took flight from penal court
Gon' find you and sideline you
Me and my cohorts
Trick your kids into believing
Their deadbeat dad really wanted to abort

Didn't get any better
Even after the judge asked Stella,
"Is he a good father?"
As she began to speak ("He's a greaaa-")
The judge intervened,
"Don't bother!"
Revoked his license, six months in the bing
And don't worry about the canteen
Because your account will have a child support lien

Judge looked at his son with a slight chuckle
And said,
"Can't wait for you to cut up in school so we can put you in a buckle"

Lil man looked at the judge with a side-eye grin:

You ain't gon' never see me or none of my friends
You got my mom believing this imperial court will be her savior
My dad taught me well and to watch my behavior
Taught me to be steadfast
Independent
And fearless
And beware of those who want me to reframe
And be bare-faced and beardless
My mama thinks her boss is my daddy
'Cause he cuts the check and speaks like Obama,
Thinks she's above 'cause my daddy's checks don't have commas
But I'm here to tell the court, that don't mean a thing to me
I have on clean clothes, fresh shoes, bills paid and well fed
PJ's, slippers and a great bookshelf on the side of my bed
Football, basketball, barbecues in the park
Horsey back rides, we even played boogie man in the dark
Homework, haircuts, and holidays are fabulous
Taught me to do things mom couldn't
Even taught me calculus

When the judge gave his decision, Mom clapped
I said *Dang*

Now I'm still waiting
30 minutes after the school bell rang
Mom what happened?
"Sorry, I had to meet with a friend
He's nice to me and he drives a Benz"

I don't care about that, Mom
I miss my dad
I don't know it all, but it didn't seem all that bad
My dad was there every day to pick me up from school
Didn't come home to an empty house and a TV dinner for food
His truck wasn't new, and the seats were a little torn
But I felt like a boss when he let me blow the air horn
Now I'm home bored cause you work more
Way past six
Running around now after school with my friends
Swearing, throwing rocks, and swinging sticks
Mad at the world and my grades on the decline
Ran away from home cause my mom's always angry
And whoops my behind
Man, oh man, I wish my dad didn't have to leave
I could tell that devil in that black robe had a trick up his sleeve
Mama's new boyfriend comes by, but we don't really speak
All he seems to care about is his car
And what him and Mom are doing this week
That's ok, I'll show them all
It ain't nothing but a thang
I heard they were accepting applications around the corner
To join a Crips or Blood gang
Sounds good to me, just might be my new play

Tattoos, a 40 cal, some drugs, and a new name
Pocket full of commas, gold ring and a chain
Mad at the world still stamped in his brain
Pulled out on anyone that brought him disdain
Late night fist fight
Stab wounds and bloody knuckles
Aggravated assault
Weapons charge
Black robe
And that same old chuckle,

"I told you one day we would put you in a buckle"

WANDERING SPIRITS

Walking through tunnels of light, darkness, happiness, and sorrow
Both eyes open with rampant visions of yesterday's horrors

Excuse me, Shadow, may I have a light?
Continue with what you felt was real yesterday
But today, well…
Today is dark again

How can this be?
Images, shadows, and figments can't exist without light
Is it me?
Tell me, is it me?
Why can't I see Tomorrow?

Dark Shadow, reveal yourself!
I know not anyone else but what I felt or saw yesterday

I hear her voice vaguely
Her vocals silenced by the tightness of her lips
Her vision distorted by yesterday's dark shadow
Her love, well…
Her love is love, but endearment has clothed itself with anxiety

Blind-siding, unwelcoming sex driving me crazy yesterday,
The other yesterday
The one that's supposed to transmute life joy light
Baby you're out of sight
For real, you are

I can't see you, Night Shadow
But I can hear you
Searching for your day star glow
Your rainbow glow
Your smile
I'm still walking because I believe in Tomorrow
Even in the absence of light in the meanwhile

Do you still want to go?
I feel like I've seen your shadow before
I'll turn the knob
Even if the *Do Not Disturb* sign is on
Invade your shadow and trip the silent alarm

JOURNEY OF A THOUGHT

Here, use my key and shine my light
It was dormant, just needed a charge....

220 volts
Stop talking, feel the spiritual jolt
Let it exhume and burn those dead bones
Cremate our shadows and use a stronger light to find
Our way back home
Heaven's Lights are always on
Just look up!

JOURNEY OF A THOUGHT

Remarkably
I've chosen to walk with myself, talk to myself, and just be
Reconfiguring the hindering traumatic experiences
that don't seem to part from me
Some self-inflicted painful addictions, situations of despair and
depressing dispositions
Blaming others for my own reckless decisions
But not all of them we can own, we can relate to broken homes
Jail, financial extortion, pregnancies and abortions
Too many of us in the house to receive a progressive portion
To succeed, not bleed and lead with anger
Escape from where when you're surrounded by danger?
And preyed upon by family and manipulative strangers
Inferior and captive religious persuasion to be Catholic or Baptist
Proved to be fooled; "Hell no!" to the chaplain
What's happening is over, four leaf and a clover
Misguided, misled, unprotected and scared
A strong shoulder to be bolder and brave a soldier
I told you I'll rise, you look surprised
I made it in spite – the traps were set tight
Noose on neck, I broke and ran; my thoughts, my plan, blueprint in
hand
A righteous demand, now take a stand
I know you can refrain from saying you can't
You will defeat no deal so climb the mountain and hurdle the hill
And strengthen your will, reinforce your skills – new thoughts, new
drill
Remove your shell, return to life; be strong, not frail
Replace your thoughts – new Heaven,
new bell that rings of joy for all to hear
Can't erase your past, Windex
New reflections, no smudges clear glass
To see right through to the beauty you are, uncover your blemishes,
reveal your scars
Head up high and capture the stars;
right now is now, you are who you are
Be proud, rejoice; you're capable and ready
So make the choice to give, to smile, and love yourself
The past is gone, what's now? What's next?
Achieve, be blessed, take back your innocence
You're perfect and more, and nothing less

INVISIBLE US

Blank pages, no ink to drip
Dry eyes, no tears to cry,
Empty space, no more lies to erase

Hear you but I can't see your face
Who are you?
What happened to what seemed like it could be?
Ok, I get it, you were only looking at me
You really don't know who I am to myself
I wanted to show you, but you keep changing your face
And running in place
I am not tired because I haven't had to chase
Just face the countless images in this invisible race
Of a place you can't even find living in your own space
Damn, and to think the world had green grass over there
With no gates, what a big mistake
Drowning frowning
Please help
Please Yelp Ten Best Solutions
Red couch can't vouch, just mental prostitution
Verbal overload revolution
Heard it all before again and then migraine contusion
The smile, pointy fangs, the lips, the pain
You felt no gain
But the juice kept pouring in your lap like lust rain
So you remained as she drained the remembrance of pain
'Til morning came, and you came and came
And screamed her name
Oh shame, oh shame
The Devil to blame
We must be the same
I denounce its name and you the same
Tomorrow, tomorrow she'll scream my name
As I too will open my door again and again

52 BLOCKS: GAME 3

The biggest game of my life
Though middle age had set in
My wife is expecting my third child
Mecca tagged me in

She entered the game without fuss or fight
Yet her premature entry would test all my might
One pound, nine ounces; I could cup her in my hands
Worried, but not scared, I knew God had a wonderful plan

Tubes, lines, machines, great doctors and nurses
Took great care of my little Angel
As I played angelic music
And read Koranic verses
Oh I prayed and prayed and stayed close to her bedside
The slant of her incubator caused her little body to slide
To our amazement, she pulled her tiny self back up
In tiny little strides

Challenge after challenge, my body grew weary
My wife was not well either
And her eyes stayed teary
Strong giant I claimed to be must conquer this challenge
Can't lose the game now
Laced up my New Balance
I'm the coach calling the plays, so I thought I was in charge
But that still small voice in my head said,

Son, I'm still Lord

Trying to understand the writing on the wall
And why my precious seed was born smaller than a baseball
Time stood still, seemed like an eternity
Couldn't hold my daughter
Felt my wife's sorrow for her premature maternity

Damn this was tough
I felt like I was in outer space
All the tubes and tape on my little angel's face
Felt so helpless and lost as a most valuable father
But you better believe I was at the hospital
Every minute, every hour

JOURNEY OF A THOUGHT

At last, the time had come
We could hold our baby girl close to our skin
She tucked her head in my chest
And looked up at me with a small grin

Oh, how beautiful was that moment we needed from the start
It kept us stronger and gave her the spark
She began to grow stronger, but not with big leaps and strides
We still had challenges and she remained inside

Four months, to be exact, before we could bring her home
Still by her bedside playing soft music from my phone
Our interactions with her grew longer each day
I held her high and close to my face

We shared energy vibrations and spoke with our souls
Her cute little face looks like mine, even her toes
Wow, is this me again?
Displaying the strength and might I need to possess
All the love and nourishment that manifested where I grew up on Vest

I was sent here for you,
Her spirit said to my heart

I came to finish the game
My sister and brother already played their part
So while you are striving to be about your Holy Circle 7
My tiny little body in the incubator
My spirit transcended from Heaven

At that moment, I understood the voices in my head:

It's time to wake up, giant, and use what you've been fed
I kept you here for 52 years
All the havoc you left behind
You could have a studio apt on a jailhouse tier

But I spared you
Because of your irregularities
And your love for family and community
You better get with it and don't blow any more
opportunities
You've done ok but you have much more talent
So I sent my Angel, Mecca, to you
To break you down and prepare you for a bigger
challenge

41

JOURNEY OF A THOUGHT

There's four quarters in this game son, have you
    forgotten?
Stop breathing so hard and stop all that snotting
Game ain't over, so keep the playbook open
Pull out your binoculars and keep on scoping

This world is suffering from fallen humanity
Nothing seems to be working and it's causing insanity
I'm preparing strong fathers whom I know can lead
Who have prepared their children well
To take care of mom if they must leave

We all can bear witness
I'm sure you watch the news
Life is getting tough
Who wants to wear political shoes?

Enough of that
I'm still in the third quarter
I'm not finished talking about my fabulous daughter
Her health got better, and it changed our mood
I will put my life on the fact
It was from the essence of her Mother's all-natural food

She grew stronger, smarter
And brilliant for her age
Nothing premature about her
I know she's a Master Sage
This little girl loves the stars, moon
And the clouds in the sky
Learned the Moorish American prayer before she was two
No lie

Past generations have been given worldly titles
Baby Boomers, Generation X
They have all been vital
You can search for the true meaning with fine tooth bristles
I don't care what anyone says
She came straight from Big Mama's Crystal

The new term of the century, must I define?
These babies are special and oh, so divine
Preparation for my work like the prophets of old
This game isn't over so I'm holding like Job

JOURNEY OF A THOUGHT

Well, my dear family, time to close my mouth
My coach from Heaven just gave me a frown and said,

Daddy what you talking about?

Yeah, yeah, yeah
She's bossy and fly and quick with her lips
Look at you crazy with her hands on her hips
I gotta go now, but I promise to tell you the rest
I knew Big Mama gave her her soul when I took her to Vest

I love you, my Angel
Thank you for the strength and your Fatherly blessings

Your Loving Father,

Steven Britt El

TONY L

My Brother
My dude
My fam
What else can I say
Other than we used to jam

Always fly, real, and about his shine
Didn't matter if his pockets were full
Or down to a dime

Fly whips
Gangster trips
The best of both worlds
Laced up
Kicks tuff
Clean cut, and waves on swirl

Yeah, we balled out and played the block in the A
In a 'bout it 'bout it fashion
Turned up so hard
Always lit and closed captioned

Vegas nights
Mayweather fights
Vanquish and Reign
No matter where we went it was like a Jay-Z song
Money Ain't a Thang

Top down
No frowns
When our crew lit up the scene
Ray Dog in the cut
Twisting up
Some of that gangsta green

Newkirk on deck
With the inspect a shoe check
Joints ain't never been seen

JOURNEY OF A THOUGHT

Imported straight from Quebec

Jay pullin' up in the tricked-out BM
Thousand-dollar sweatsuit on
Talking 'bout he just left the gym

B Mo D slid in
With a west side friend
Cartier on and a watch yo' chick grin

My man Don moving through the spot
With a bankroll like a knot
Told the bartender keep pouring it up
And she bet not stop

G O got us laughing
'Cause he lit with that smooth…
The hustla flow
Don't see him that much but been fam from the door

The youngest of the crew always come through
In shape and ready to flex
The crew nicknamed him Superman PJ 90X

Definitely can't forget Nancy
Our sister and Queen
Made us all look like late night snacks
Being sexy with the team

Don't mean no harm if I didn't add your name
Just started writing to ease some of this pain

We gon' miss you my brother
The link that made part of this chain
I'm certain your two strong sons
And your beautiful granddaughter
Will continue your legacy and your name

Rest In Peace
And ball way above Heaven's skies
And one thing to remember
We're friends for life
Because Spirit Man can break no ties

Your Brother 4 Life

45

MOON LOVE

Mystic energy mixed
with a misty summer night rain
| Soft music playing | I'm stargazing |
Mesmerized as I fashion you from Goddess
clouds | So amazing, so alluring | All of you so
contagious | Spelled your name with the stars |
Beautiful eyes, angel arms | Float to me overpowering
scents | Arabian night storm | Ooohh so warm | Heavenly
charmed | Melanin infused translucent cosmic garb | And
your eyes | Your eyes, like staring into a blissful Milky Way
| Planetarium | Uncontrollable, my planets collide |Oh what a
moon ride | Flaming meteorites our candlelight | Craters for
cuddling, spooning and snuggling; high altitude | Long
journey | Extra fuel in my tank baby | Prepare for
combustion | Galactic eruption | Terrestrial
insemination |Tantra sex awaited antici-
pation | Welcome home, love | I
was just staring at the stars,
thinking about you

Let's take a vacation

RIGHT HERE

Can I reach what I see so far out of touch?
You tell me to reach far the stars
Yet I need a rocket to go to Mars
Why am I looking up?
I own gravity
Air and earth
The earth we birth
Our journey we curse
That evolution didn't come first
Prophets and stop it
The manuscript has been written and preordained
How dare we utter His Holy Name
And not reclaim, refrain?
Chains, chains – a repetitious disdain
For truth
The salvation of our youth
Lost in a kiss and tell booth
A diabolical blood line of Jessie Booth
And his poor unrighteous ungodly false deities and troops
March on
Be sworn in, born in old spirit adhesively
Majestically and infinitely
Defiantly
We must stand in command
Steadfast
And fearless
We march united
Right here
Adherently
In the Spirit of True Man

FLESH DEEP

Four hundred plus years of recycled lies
Ropes
Chains
And pain
I wrote letters to my selves
But they were undelivered, again
And again
One was to my God
And the other to my Devil
Instead of mailing again
I went to sleep with a shovel
I was told if I dig beneath the rocky soil I would find my lost treasure
Night after night
Year after year
I dug so deep I still can't measure
Finally, I arrived
To a plane that was dark, hot, and cold
And my own ancient shadow said,

Man, you're bold
I'm kinda busy right now
With part of your captive soul
But since you dug so deep
I will reveal the untold:
Been waiting on you
What took you so long?
Every test you've failed and repeated
Kept you away from your throne
But I'm not your enemy
What you've been taught is wrong
The only people in this game are you
And yourself
If you want to kill your devil
It's not done in the flesh
I'm just a tester
I'm not the final gate keeper
You need to keep digging
Conquer your unconscious grim reaper

So, I went back to sleep

This time with my shovel and a ladder
I dug down so deep I got madder
And madder

JOURNEY OF A THOUGHT

I arrived in a place that was peaceful and serene
Unlike any physical plain I had ever seen
Was this an illusion the devil placed in my mind?
Or is this the sacred place where I begin my new climb?
As I began to climb from the depths of the dead
The light got brighter
And a strong voice said,

You've dug down so deep
I will remove the mark from your brain
The dirt you left behind will relinquish your pain
The climb to the top will be a battle for a giant
Pay close attention
Strive hard and be less defiant
I've equipped you with all the wisdom and secrets
For generations to come
On the way back up kill your devil
Or I'll inflict your sons
Your fight is far from over
So resist temptation
You're starting all over on a stronger foundation
Heaven comes with a price
But hell is a lot cheaper
So be a strong father
So your daughters aren't seekers
And your devil was right
He is not the gatekeeper
Neither am I, you're your own grim reaper
The deeper you dig the higher you will climb
If you come down here again
Your soul will be mine

REMEDY

If I could heal all my sisters
I would do it with a soft whisper
I would say thank you for my life
Thank you for being my
Mother/Friend/Wife

Thank you for your beautiful essence
Thank you for your support
And forgiveness
Even after I failed my manly lessons

Thank you for love
Hovering over our family like angels above

Thank you for your care
Soft touch, pretty smile
Straight, kinky, and curly hair

Thank you for your sweetness
Even when you're upset
You practice a polite tongue and meekness

Thank you for your intimacy
Deserves to be honored and upheld
Legitimately

Thank you for my offspring
My children have inspired me as a father
To do what I must do by all means

Thank you for civilization
Your life-giving dedication
Birth of all nations
God's gift to Creation
The Manifestation
Of all life's anticipations
And determinations

Thank you
For just naturally being a phenomenal sensation...
The Universe needs to respect, honor, love
And show more appreciation
For the true queen goddess warriors on all planet life stations

52 BLOCKS: GAME 4

I am your father too

Is a representation
Of a great friend whose spirit traveled on to a higher destination
Her spirit so beautiful and friendship divine
There was no way my family would ever leave you behind
Faith, how beautiful, and that be your name
As fate would have it, you're now part of our gang
I can only imagine the hurt you feel from the loss of your mother
So thankful to be here
And for you to gain two sisters and a brother
I love when we hang out for dinner or lunch
When we're all together we look like the Brady Bunch
But that's all good, I wouldn't change it for a million nickels
I still remember taking you and Rocco out for ice cream and popsicles
Seems like yesterday
Forever
But not far apart
I've watched you grow up and you're exceedingly smart
Your mother raised you well and fashioned you to succeed
I will always be in your life for whatever you need
I know you're so proud of your daughter Ms. Angel Felicia
No one can replace a mother, but Faith did inherit Mrs. Alicia
I'm thankful Faith has another person that can see her through
She needs that because there's certain things a father just can't do
At any rate and whatever the season
I'm available around the clock for any reason
I know you're in college now but don't be a stranger
And you better believe I'll come for anyone who puts you in any danger
You're still my little girl that loved going to Dave and Busters
We've traded them in for Spondivits crab leg clusters
The most important thing I want you to know
Your mom is very special to me
I miss her creative flow
She gave me great books to read
I read them when I am alone
I know she's smiling from Heaven
Happy to know you have a second home

We love you very much Faith

Your Loving Father,

Steven Britt-El

51

DOUBLE EXPOSURE

Life could be a movie drama
Every living being scarred by human
And inhumane trauma
Crooked smiles
A thousand miles
And no red carpet exposure
Pretentious thoughts left on life's stage
Now here comes the bulldozer
Screenplays of happy days
Like a misty summer mirage
Pick me!
Pick me!
I can act
And swarmed the stage in a barrage
We all are acting
Non-contracting
Looking for the big prize
A Golden Globe
A green silk robe
And the Hollywood shuck and jive
Read your lines
I see it blind
You mean to tell me you can't hear those lies?
Reverse the game and live it plain
By playing the role you feel
The layers of lies
Will flee like flies
No need to roll the reel
The motion picture will never fit ya
No need to act at all
When the phone rings for real for real
You still won't hear the call
So stop pretending
Make up the ending
By creating a new genuine start
And when you're thinking you're acting out
And can no longer play the part
Take off your mask
Dismiss your cast
And return the Tin Man's heart

SOCIAL MEDIA

Ha ha,
That's funny
Growing up – no social media
Facebook, IG or Wikipedia
Cat in the Hat
101 Dalmatians
I bet you I can beat you reading them

Outside was fun
Clothes pin, some wood, a rubber band –
Top Gun
No Build a Bear
We played two-square
Hopscotch, jump rope and jacks
No fancy parks
Played tag 'til dark
Ate watermelon for a snack
Hawaii trips to take a dip
Man please…
Plastic pool in our backyard

School yard b-ball
Boys Club had it all
And was the place that made us tough
We had so much fun shooting our top guns
We didn't know life was rough

Catch a girl, kiss a girl
Sounds funny, but was probably my favorite game
Except when you catch the ugly girl
The kiss turns into shame

My cousins and I built bikes
From scraps we scrounged from hood to hood
We tricked them out and fixed them right
To us they rode just as good
A Green Machine was not on the scene
Our Big Wheels were made of wood
Barbecue grill we got our wheels
And we used the rods for axels
I know you don't believe me but ask Cousin Co
He'll tell you my stories are factual

JOURNEY OF A THOUGHT

No summertime trips
Old mattresses for flips
Buddy sneakers on our feet
Here comes the snow cone truck y'all!
Let's ante up for a treat
You got a nickel, I got a dime
So the big piece of pickle is mine
That's ok, I don't want to share
It's hot so I bought a Vess Lemon Lime
Big cuz is smarter
Bossed up with two quarters
Pushed us out of the way
Her fifty cents spent further
She got a Buzz Daddy, seeds, and a Payday

Super-hot day, kids are frowning
And nobody's really that vibrant
Until the neighborhood mechanic pulled out a big wrench
To unleash the fire hydrant
Splash, SPLASH
Feet cut on glass
Board in the middle, create a strong blast
Run too close it may blast you all way to Cass…

We had a free water park on our block
No summertime budget for Disney
Just plain old Chain of Rocks
No trampoline
A fun rusty swing and a host of neighborhood friends
No expensive movies
Paper bag popcorn, Charlie's Chicken
And a night at the drive-in with my cousins was groovy

I can write a thousand-page novel
But the first page would allow you to understand in an instant
We had way more fun than kids of today
Because their social media have created a gap
And social distance
I know the world is evolving and life must change
But I wouldn't change a thing from whence the block I came

YELLOW GODDESS

The power of her silence
She vibrates radiant love over violence
Her sweetness calms the strongest ocean waves to quietness

Sunrise morning beauty casts the most alluring spells
Earthly men who tried to tame her failed

No disguise when she arrives
Skin so beautiful
Spiritual frame so fine
Yellow adorned every curve of her body and every line

The wind spoke her presence Fragrance of her power and femininity
Captivating and radiant

I wanted to know her
Behold her
Ingest her energy like food
Her grace and the golden glow from her face spoke the words
I'm not for any ordinary dude

Her strong wind blew past
As I took my last glance at this beautiful Goddess
Fading away into the shadows of the ocean
Asking myself could I have tamed her, or shamed
My inner man for lack of spiritual love and devotion

MAN DOWN

This shit be going crazy
Trying to relate
Debate
Stand tall and not forsake
Heaven knows we need a new master template

The murders
High hurdles and ruthless deserters
No need for news reporters
We're live spectators
Have seen it all
No need to blog
It's thick like fog
Self-hate is real
No love to feel
What happened to us?
Why must we kill what matters the most?

All caught up on names
Is he this?
He ain't folk
But your father, my father, our mother – no joke
Birth your daughter; my aunt, your cousins came first
Grandmother
Big Unc, niece and nephew
It really doesn't matter whose life is in the hearse

It's yours
It's mine
We're connected by time
Rewind, rewind
Research, you'll find
What's yours is mine, and ours to keep
To share in love
Not kill, not weep
Damn this hard

I'm scared
What happens next?

Just when the mountain seemed possible to climb
Life fell lifeless
Out of context

You sank my battleship
What happened to DJ Khalid?
We're the best
All that sacrifice and my own image
Stole my promise
Destroyed all those connected promises
Bloodshed, yellow tape
Blue sheet, red stain
Teenage initiation
Neighborhood death train

Can someone please enlighten me?
What's wrong with our name?
Why you hate me?
Why you can't see?
My son, your son
My daughter, your daughter
    My pain, your pain

Our mothers traded shoes and dreamed of us
When they laughed and giggled on the playground
Watching our fathers play basketball before we got here
No one measured
Our little hope was a giant treasure
Our effort was love
Pride
Unity
A Black Power Community

What happened to being cut from a certain cloth?
A fabric of humanity
Not a rag, flag stained with murder
Self-hate, raw vanity
Human weapons of destruction
Is it not time for reconstruction`n?

YEAH YOU

So, I'm sitting here all alone, day dazing
Twinkle in your beautiful eyes stargazing
Please pardon my rude behavior
Butter soft golden skin
I'm wondering what flava
Can I come just a little bit closer?
Wet your pretty lips
Strawberry Mimosa
Heard you tell your friend you had very uneventful day
Life's about to change sunshine, tell me,
What's your name?
Gorgeous to my eyes, bank account, ball lock and chain
Had a daydream, didn't even know your birth name
Ocean front crib, two kids in the same domain
Read you like a book, bit your lips, sexy, crossed your legs
Breakfast in the morning – lox and bagels, maybe scrambled eggs
I'm a King, got a throne
Need a Queen,
Can I take you home?
Your smile growing bigger, piercing eyes
Put away your phone
Sexy, soft spoken, gorgeous teeth
Damn, you make me moan
It's about time to cross the line, grabbed her by her hand
Summertime dress, pretty toes
May I have this dance?
Music just right, held her tight
Think she felt my man
Damn
She's out of sight

She looked me in my eyes, closed her eyes
Fell into a trance as if to say,

I'm yours and you're mine
I want to take this chance
Truth in your eyes so divine
Didn't waste my time with corny pickup lines
Gentleman's approach, intellectual
Smell great, and you're fine
I was gazing too
Gucci frames sort of hid my eyes
Your deep voice and dancing
Lit a fire near my upper thighs

Queen and a bee need a King
I want to feel your sting
Honeycomb hideout
Can we ride out?
Can we make it a real dream?
Love at first sight; candlelight
And a promise ring

Ten years later
Baby girl, puppy, home, and a swing
No need to second guess
I must confess to you
I'm thankful we're on the same team

SOUL REBEL

Balled up fist to cuffs
WTF
Black Panther Movement
To Black Lives Matter
Soft as cotton ball puffs
Social video pros
Standing around mean muggin'
With weak elbows
Making cowardly excuses for why they didn't throw blows
To aid and assist their fellow brothers and sisters
Who were being maliciously robbed of their Divine Soul
Murdered in the street
As if the murderer deserved life over me
So cold
How dare you take something so precious that God granted thee
As if you own this world?
You are a public servant
But a disgrace
And to hell you deserve
As the old saying goes,
"You will reap what you sow"
Before the end
And whoever sent you to do the dirty work will reap the same
And their next of kin

These words aren't from hate
But I am quite disturbed
Too see my brother's life being taken
On a dirty street curb
What most bothers my heart
Is no one did a thing…
And now you want to march
Throw rocks, loot, dance, and sing
We say enough is enough
Need they show us more?
They won't give a fuck about us
Until we start sending them to the morgue
Our anger must be redirected
Controlled and organized

JOURNEY OF A THOUGHT

Move in unison militantly
And with some race pride

Pay attention and understand
You're not just dealing with what your eyes and videos presume
Most of these missions are premeditated in a precinct board room
The evil of the evils
Are commissioned to carry out these murders and hate crimes
Yeah, they publicly get fired
But they don't go to jail
Or lose their pension or a dime
They wanted you to witness what they did
As if we were still in slavery ...
And lo and behold
We prove them right
Every time
By being cowards and possessing fear
No heart or bravery

What are we living for if we're not going to stay divinely connected?
Who will they kill next?
Any one of us could be selected

WHERE'S MY FATHER?

Little innocent boys and girls we create
Without any hesitation nor sexual debate
That moment of desire
Our mothers warned us about playing with fire
Abandonment more than a mistake
Truly a blatant unnatural disgrace

Ready for the world
Brown eyes, curly curls
Little toes
And runny noses
We chose to create
How dare we forsake '
And claim divinity a mistake?

You should be ashamed
To look at your own reflection
And blame it on inadequate protection
Against the fence!
But in defense of the innocent
All proud fathers stand up and represent
The defenseless

We stand with a new demand
For an everlasting life glance
A right now demand

God told you His plan in our old land
And now you so bold to believe
You have the power to deal
Your own hand
Strong Goliath
Full of riot
Fearless fathers
Please
Let's take a stance

52 BLOCKS MVF (MOST VALUABLE FATHER)

Thank you seeds, for all your time
Pass back the rock
It's time for Dad to shine
I will give each of you a no-look pass
You've all been well taught
So bank it off the glass

Swoosh Swoosh
Was the sound when the ball hit the net
The ref grabbed the ball as I hand-checked myself
Crossed over once, dribbled through my legs three times
Couldn't shake this dude, his steps too divine
Leaped high above the rim with my hand over one eye
Slammed the ball so hard thunder roared from the sky
My children went crazy and said, "WOW, our dad can fly!"
Indeed, I can
I use my third eye

Believe in yourself
And always be diligent
I hope I wasn't too hard on you
I was only being militant
Where I come from, we had to be strong
Because most of our fathers were absent or gone

I'm 52 now, and they say I'm in the middle
The timer is ticking but I solved the riddles
What I want from you three is to take care of each other
Sherita you're the oldest so look out for your little brother
Rocco, you left the house smooth like a whisper
Always protect and take care of your big and your baby sisters
Stay close in life as family should
Never be the little engines that didn't think they could

Texting is good but I would rather hear your voices
I brought you in the game, so you have no other choices
I don't care if you're a mile away, or fifty
Disobey my wishes and you will get the switchy

We are blood and bone
Flesh and flesh
So stay close to each other
As your father I expect nothing but the best

JOURNEY OF A THOUGHT

You all came into the game and put points on the board
So keep the game clean and practice no discord
I promise if you practice love and follow the rules
As brothers and sisters, you will not lose
So trust my judgment and carry out my wishes
Mecca you will soon be old enough to wash some dishes
Rocco, you're gone but still on the team
Pop got plenty of work when you're back on the scene
Ree Ree you're laughing because you are the oldest
The job I have for you is definitely the coldest
You are responsible for unlocking the secrets
Go get the bag and make sure nobody peeps it
Dump your cell phone before you jump in the car
Make sure it's old, we don't need no OnStar
Pick up your brother with lights on low dim
Grab his cell phone and remove his sim
Cross over the bridge and turn next to the tracks
Lil' sis will be waiting, she'll jump right in the back
Keep your speed steady, no need for alarm
Drive to the country, ditch the car in the red barn
A Jeep will be waiting for your final destination
Stop all that playing, no time for hesitation
You're one step away from completing our mission
Rocco, stop trying to give your rendition
Your sisters have strict orders to follow my plan
Mecca wake up and grab your big brother's hand
Ride is over but a flight awaits you
The island you're going to looks like a big horseshoe
No need to worry, when you land you will be safe
Go in the house, put the bag in the safe
Turn on the TV and relax for a while
Make sure you keep an eye on my third child
Ree Ree, you made it to the final retreat
Be proud of yourself, you fought through defeat

Now take a seat in those three chairs
The steps you hear is me on the stairs
You all looked surprise when I turned on the light
Couldn't leave this world until I knew you were alright
Always be close, my dear children
I love all of you with every inch of my life
In life and in spirit

Your Loving Father,

Steven Britt-El

ONE DAY

Today
Is the day I sing a perfect song
Today
Is the day I am me alone and I have no uncertainties
Today
Is the day I see myself unchallenged by judgement
Today
I see myself thinking only of me
Today
I see myself through my own tentacles
Today
I feel my own heartbeat
Today
I tell myself I'm priceless
Today
I tell myself I don't need
Today
I tell myself I matter
Today
I love the flaws I don't have
Today
I tell myself I don't care what you think
Today
I tell myself you're not better than I
Today
I tell myself I can be myself without you
Today
I exist in the perfect me
Today
I found my happy
Today
Today
Today

CONTROL 2X

Anniversary but not a celebration
A holiday bail out pandemic dollar day for some
But everyone didn't get none
Blessed are the souls that still rise under the sun
PPP loans, SBA's, 1040's, Schedule C's and Zoom parties
Got us drinking out the Hennessy bottle
They even reintroduced the Colt 45 forty
Don't forget to pour out a splash for our dearly departed
Damn, what's next?
Can't seem to catch the vibe
All touchless outside
The sun and the moon out at the same damn time
Wind blowing atmospheric homicide
We gotta be supernatural to still be alive
Fuck what you heard on the news
Pay attention and look to the sky
Those unidentifiable objects are the return of the Jedi
Zombie apocalypse, race war atrocities
Capitalism and mutiny
Presidential hypocrisy
Shit vanished from the news
But 30 years have passed and we still talking about Rodney King
Don't sleep, don't dream
We all saw it live on the dumb you down screen
Did I take what?
The Covid vaccine?
Maann... I'm a man pulled straight from the ground
Born to live eternally, you can't see God's Crown?
I see yours, his, and hers – halos, angel wings
And hear the voice of The Master
Warning us to roll down our sleeves
That shot could be a genetic disaster
Lack of knowledge, mental programming,
And European college; remember, they're the same humankind
That raped our mothers and killed our forefathers
But who am I to tell you not to go get the shot, man
Go pop your collar
I'll holla
I'm staying clear of those kill you slow scams
Y'all please forgive my pen; I'm trying to catch the rhythm of the stroke
News flash! News flash! I heard Jim Crow was still woke
I be damned, this shit has to be a jokie joke
Remember the old saying, the devil is a lie

Will everyone please turn to their neighbor
And ask who they think the lying devil is
Don't front, don't be shy
I'll tell you who it is, and he wasn't expelled from the sky
Not even underground, they stand up every day
Looking you dead in your eyes
Tell Li Vision lies, plasma Wi-Fi 80"
Illuminating brain cuffs and verbal pesticides
Stay tuned, stay tuned – 500 channels can't escape this devil's ride
And we pay for the cable recycled repetitive lies
Entertainment my ass; deaf, dumb, and blind
Reject reflect we created all this shit
Now let's move to the front of the line
Damn, we can't just yet; Got another news flash
Big brother sending crash dummies to whoop the Chinese's ass
But it won't last
The Communists already got their foot deep in Biden's ass
Black Lives Matter
However
Their defining process is far from what black lives perceive
You bet not for one second believe
The US hasn't amalgamated with the Chinese
We matter; of course we matter
Every nation feeds off our blood equity
King and Queen trajectory
Knowledge of self, strong genetic melanin masterminds
Bearing high IQ's, mental telepathy ability, slam dunk agility
Race multipliers, odds-defiers; to sum it all up:
We're walking gods
Atomic energy clothed with a soul that has endured hell's fire
We ain't gon' never expire
Send them all back to the land and caves
Of the uncivilized and the undesirables
Time to take control
Panic and pandemic introduced by wolves in sheep's clothes
Rise up and remember they plan our demise a century two-fold
Everyone you see doesn't possess a real soul

ABOUT THE AUTHOR

Born in St. Louis
Universal game
Standing firmly on my square
Last of the truest, must I proclaim

Blessed to be a son,
Husband and a father
Uncle, nephew, brother,
And some say an Islamic scholar

JOURNEY OF A THOUGHT

Lived in many cities
Adapted well
Elevated to high plains
Refused to fail

Educated on the toughest streets, avenues and boulevards
Escaped some living hells
Tattoos cover my scars

Nine lives for cats
How many you think are allotted for a brother man?
The poems will reveal
I've lived more lives than your average Superman

I was in a dark place when I wrote these poems
My life was plagued with confusion, pain, and instabilities
My focus went to sports reading, writing, roller skating
And exploring life's possibilities

All praise is due to the Most High
I've been so blessed
Fortunately my key still unlocks the door
To a home where grandmother said, "always do your best!"

My journey to redemption was a battle from within
Didn't want to die living
Or the coroner to notify my next of kin

JOURNEY OF A THOUGHT

So travel along and learn through me
The messages in these poems may heal you internally

I searched for help I fought and I sought
Redemption took place
With one man's journey of a thought

Made in the USA
Columbia, SC
13 June 2022

61597027R00046